THE HARP
OF BRANDISWHIERE

narrative and suite for Celtic harp
inspired by tales of the legendary harper

music composed by SYLVIA WOODS

story by SYLVIA WOODS

based on an original idea by TOM WOODS

edited by DON SNYDER

illustrations by STEVE DUGLAS

WOODS MUSIC

Thanks to:
   Tommy and Marjorie for their editorial assistance
   Mother and Father for their vital help
   Pam and Tommy for their patience and understanding
   Don for everything

Music typeset by Robert H. K. Lau
Book typeset by Computerized Shorthand Systems
Cover art direction by Peter Green
Illustrations by Steve Duglas

The harp and flute arrangements of "In the Forest" and
"Brandiswhiere's Triumphant Return"
are available on sheet music from the Sylvia Woods Harp Center.

The Harp of Brandiswhiere recording on Tonmeister Records
is available on CD or mp3 files from the Sylvia Woods Harp Center.

Sylvia Woods Harp Center
www.harpcenter.com

Published by Woods Music & Books
P.O. Box 3574, Lihue, Hawaii 9676 USA

First Edition 1982
Second Edition 2004
Third Edition 2023

ISBN 0-9602990-2-5

This book is dedicated to Tommy,
who knew and remembered Brandiswhiere

TABLE OF CONTENTS

A Guide to the Suite:

The musical suite and story of THE HARP OF BRANDISWHIERE are woven together to form the complete version of the legend. The music in this book is in the correct sequence for the tale, and can be played on harp or piano. It is also available on album or cassette, performed on the Celtic harp by Sylvia Woods. When reading the story, it is suggested that you stop whevever you reach ∿♩∿, and listen to the music indicated.

A Word to Harpers:

Many of the pieces in this book are marked "Rubato". This means that they should not be played in strict rhythmic time. Instead, certain notes within the measures or phrases can be lengthened or shortened to create a more flowing musical expression. I suggest that you use my album THE HARP OF BRANDISWHIERE to guide you in this interpretation.

DIALOGUE WITH A BROOK was composed for metal-strung harp, although it can also be played on nylon-strung harps. It has no sharps or flats. In all the other pieces, the Fs are always sharped. LAMENT and GOURENSPUR have additional sharps, and the pedals or sharping levers should be set at the beginning of these pieces, and will not need to be altered until the piece is completed. There are no lever changes in the middle of any of the pieces.

In GYPSY MIRAGE some of the Ds are sharped, and some are left natural. On non-pedal harps, sharp the D which is one octave and one note above middle C, and leave the other Ds natural. You will not need to change any levers during the piece. Pedal harpists will need to sharp and natural the Ds as needed.

If there are any musical terms or notations with which you are not familiar, you should be able to find them in a good music dictionary. All harmonics are written where played.

I hope you enjoy playing THE HARP OF BRANDISWHIERE SUITE. If you have any questions or comments, please feel free to write to me.

Sylvia Woods
Email: sylvia@harpcenter.com
www.harpcenter.com

PROLOGUE

Harpers will tell you the Legend of the Island. They say it lies far away in a remote part of the ocean known only to them. A special island of breathtaking beauty. An island of perpetual peace. It is the island of eternal Spring.

As they tell it, the island was created eons ago during a dark and troubled epoch. Then sorcerers and magicians ruled the world and wrestled each other constantly for control. No place was safe from their malevolent influence, no land unscathed by the ravages of their wars. Beauty, art, and music seemed to be all but banished from the world.

Yet amid all this turmoil, one lone harper persevered, and through the magic of his music, protected himself as he traveled the land. A lifetime of wandering honed his instinct for survival, sharpened his artistic senses, broadened the scope and power of his music, and made his magic as strong as that of any of the wizards.

As an old man, he tired of the constant struggle, and decided to leave a legacy which would influence the world long after he was gone. So he sat down with his harp, and summoning all of his magical powers, and concentrating all of his musical prowess, began to play.

He played the image he saw in his mind: the image of an island. A special place filled with good people, and beautiful things, and music. A source of music. A home for music. The more he played, the more involved he became. And as he played faster, he seemed to melt into the image even as the image began to take on the appearance of reality. Faster and harder he played, giving himself totally to this musical frenzy.

And the island began to be.

His fingers flew on the strings creating powerful chords that became steep white cliffs rising from an azure sea. On and on he played. With intricate melodies, he shaped beautiful deep forests, flower filled meadows, and flowing brooks and waterfalls. He decreed that it would always be Spring on the island, Winter would never come. With a shower of magical notes he populated it with birds and animals and a race of people who would grow to love their tranquil and isolated life.

Still he played on with abandon, his very being becoming the music itself. His ancient eyes gleamed as he beheld the tangible manifestation of his most noble dream.

This island was to be a haven for harpers, and they must be protected. To keep them safe and secure, he summoned his last ounce of melodic energy, and with a mighty crescendo, he cloaked his creation in a shroud of invisibility.

As the final chord faded away, there stood a wondrous magical island: magnificent, yet invisible.

And the old harper was gone. ⌣♩⌣

⌣♩⌣ THE LEGEND

Chapter 1

The isle of Spring is not large. If one were to mount one of the ponies that roam freely through the grasses, it would be a full day's journey from one end of the isle to the other, filled with an abundance of wondrous delights for the senses. The warm golden sunlight filters through the verdant leaves to the fragrant flowers that fill the forest floor. Colorful birds converse from the treetops, and gentle animals graze and play in the grassy meadows. Rich fertile fields and fruitful well-kept orchards offer the traveler a succulent assortment of tantalizing tastes. The rivers run merrily over rocks and waterfalls, and stand quietly in clear calm pools. Everywhere is the spectacular scenery of Spring. ◡♩◡

Spring is eternal on the isle. For the Legend states that if Winter ever comes, the island will become visible and be just as vulnerable to evil, and be governed by the same natural laws as the rest of the world. Winter would also bring death and destruction to the isle, and put an end to the peaceful and tranquil existence of its people.

But Spring has never shown signs of diminishing, and for centuries now, harpers have used the island as a retreat and meeting place. They are the only visitors, for theirs is the only feasible mode of transportation to the invisible isle. A harper can travel to any location, as long as he knows the tune for that specific place. He forms an image of his destination in his mind, plays the tune that duplicates it, and is immediately transported to that site.

Of the many wonderful tales told about this unique island, one of the favorites is "The Harp of Brandiswhiere". At the time of this story, two harpers, Brandiswhiere and Telena, lived on the isle with the other people of the forest.

Brandiswhiere had just completed his many years of formal training and apprenticeships and had achieved the rank of Master Harper. He was still young and idealistic, and anxious to practice all the varied skills of his craft. He had been the most promising of the harp students, and therefore was sent to be the resident harper of the isle: a position of highest honor.

Telena was a young woman who was studying the harp under Brandiswhiere's excellent guidance. She had wanted to be a harper from as early as she could remember. As a child she had fashioned toy harps from sticks and vines; her dreams filled with harps and adventures.

There was much to learn to become a harper. First, there was the technique of playing the instrument: tuning, proper hand position and finger movement, and the countless exercises for speed, accuracy, tone, and expression.

Secondly, there were many songs and tunes to remember: light songs of love and laughter, and somber songs of sorrow and grief; tunes of triumphs and victories, and those of tragedy and defeat. Harpers were the keepers of the history of mankind, and the many story songs must be learned word for word as they had been passed down for centuries from one harper to another.

But the music was only part of the harpers' repertoire. They also could perform magic. As a harper played a tune, he wove moving visual images with the music, making his stories come alive to be seen and felt, as well as heard. Harpers could evoke any emotion in their audience: laughter and joy, tears, grief, love and tenderness, even jealousy or hate. Their music could stop quarrels, ease heartaches, and even cause those who listened to fall into a deep sleep. Thus was the magic of their music.

Each harper made his harp from the hardwoods of the island's forest, and endowed it with as many magical powers as he could. These powers were quite diverse: some harps could be played only by the harper who made them, and other harps could sometimes play on their own with no human assistance. Harps could be attuned to the fundamental vibrations of nature, so that they would alert the harper to abnormal variations, including the presence of danger.

Brandiswhiere was truly a master of all of the harpers' skills. He could even make music out of Nature, herself. He coaxed music from the vines that hung down from the trees like leafy harp strings: played the ripples in a brook so that they made beautiful watery melodies.

Brandiswhiere greatly enjoyed having Telena as an apprentice. Every morning he'd teach her some new tune or technique, which she would then practice all afternoon. She was very quick, and would often have mastered the new ability before the sun had set. Many evenings they played duets by firelight, their harps blending in perfect harmonies. Or perhaps they'd sing an epic ballad from days of old; the story unfolding with verse following verse until late into the night.

Telena and Brandiswhiere had become close friends during their months together, with the music being an added bond between them. They learned to read each other's musical thoughts, and through their harps could communicate without words.

Chapter 2

One afternoon after Telena had gone into the forest to practice, Brandiswhiere's thoughts were suddenly interrupted by the feeling that she was frantically calling to him. Her communication was unclear, but full of fear and foreboding; even as he received it she seemed to be rapidly getting farther away. Brandiswhiere's reply echoed back to him unreceived, and he was alarmed that he could no longer sense Telena's whereabouts. It was as though she had vanished. Brandiswhiere picked up his harp and played the tune of her favorite practice spot, but she was not there. He quickly checked the other clearings, and then began searching through the dense underbrush. As he searched he became increasingly aware of an evil presence which seemed to permeate the entire forest.

Brandiswhiere followed the flow of the stream, and even looked behind the veil of the waterfall. He inquired of everyone he met if they knew where Telena might be, but no one had seen her. The men began to join the search. As darkness fell, they lit their torches and spread out to cover as much of the island as possible. They searched throughout the moonlit night, but found no trace of Telena.

As the morning star faded and dawn brought its first light colors to the sky, the men wearily returned. They were very worried. During all the generations since the island was first created, nothing like this had ever happened. Nothing had ever come to challenge or disrupt their peaceful existence. But now, an unnatural and unwanted presence pervaded the island. For the first time, evil had come to their land of Spring.

Brandiswhiere decided what must be done. He would summon the other harpers from distant lands, and together they would surely find Telena. With new resolve he played the tune of the oldest and wisest harper's home, expecting to be transported there, as he had been so many times before. But nothing happened. This was very strange. Just last week he had visited the ancient man, and he was certain he was playing the tune correctly. He played it again: and again nothing happened. He tried the tunes for locations of other harpers, but none of them were effective. No matter what tunes he tried, he couldn't move off of the island. Some powerful force was blocking him, preventing his magic from summoning assistance.

A great sense of dread came over Brandiswhiere. He perceived the evil force at work in the forest, and he knew that it must have somehow captured Telena. He would hold off the search for her, for he felt certain she would not be found until this power was vanquished and expelled from the island. Until then, she was lost. He could not bring himself to consider that she might have been killed and lost to him forever. He would find and fight the unseen foe, and bring his Telena back to his home and his heart. Brandiswhiere realized that he loved Telena more than anyone in the world, but had never admitted this even to himself. They were lovers, yet they had not known it.

As Brandiswhiere contemplated what he should do, he heard the notes of a shepherd's flute drifting through the early morning air from beyond the misty meadows. The music was sad and mournful, mirroring Brandiswhiere's inner feelings. Soon the notes of his harp blended with the flute in a lament for Telena. ᴖ♩ᴖ

Chapter 3

When Telena had walked into the forest to practice on that fateful afternoon, she had heard a strange rhythmic music drifting through the trees. It was unlike any tune she had ever known. Intrigued by the whistles and jangling tambourines, she followed the hypnotic sounds deeper into the forest until she came upon a band of gypsies around a blazing bonfire. The brightly colored skirts of the women swirled in mesmerizing movements as they danced to the musicians' melodies, and their shadows jumped and frolicked on the trees. Telena was fascinated by the sights and sounds, for she had never imagined that there were gypsies on the island. One of the smiling men beckoned her to join the circle of musicians, and soon the strains of her harp mingled with the intricate gypsy rhythms. ◡♩◡

After an hour of festive playing, Telena decided to enter into the dancing to give her tired fingers a bit of a rest. She gently placed her harp in a nest-like tangle of vines beneath a leafy tree, and started towards the whirling dancers. Suddenly, something was not right. She couldn't place what it was, but as soon as she had let go of her harp, things had changed. The colors looked less vibrant, as if they were slowly fading. The music was getting quieter, although the musicians seemed to be playing with as much intensity as before. As Telena watched, everything grew misty and then all movement stopped. The air was suddenly very still, and the gypsies became almost transparent, like a mirage. Telena's harp and the rest of the forest looked as they always had, but the gypsy camp was like a faded ghostly painting. As Telena reached out to pick up her harp, she found that her arm wouldn't move. Her whole body was as motionless as the gypsies. She looked at her hand, and realized with horror that she could see right through it. Telena had become part of an illusion, and she was trapped. She called out to Brandiswhiere, but her voice made no sound. The illusion continued to fade, taking her along with it. And soon both she and the illusion had totally disappeared from the forest scene.

◡♩◡ GYPSY MIRAGE

Chapter 4

Gourenspur sat in his cave-like dwelling, his evil mind plotting his next move. Even though he was a very powerful wizard, he could not see the invisible isle of Spring; but he felt it was very near to the stark, rocky island he occupied.

Gourenspur had once been much sought after by wicked kings and wealthy scoundrels, for his reputation in the black arts of sorcery was unsurpassed. But no one had seen or heard from him in many years. There were rumors that he had been in a battle with a rival wizard and had been killed, or perhaps turned into a toad or some other such unsavory creature.

Parts of this rumor were true. He had battled another wizard and had been defeated. However, instead of killing Gourenspur, or employing one of the more common wizardly spells, the victorious sorcerer cast a curse on him which was in effect worse than death, for it placed the key to Gourenspur's destruction in Gourenspur's hands. His own magic would be his downfall. The curse stated that if one of Gourenspur's spells was ever countered or nullified by the magic of another wizard or any other magical being, then he would be destroyed: his spells would be broken and his powers lost forever.

And so, with much anxiety, Gourenspur discretely hid himself away on this bleak, rocky island, and did not use his magic for several years. He was in constant fear that any magic he performed would be countered, and would annihilate him.

Gradually, he began to realize that by letting his fear overpower him, he was already destroyed. He began to experiment with new spells and effects that had never been seen before, and that he felt surely would be invincible. He knew the abilities of most of the sorcerers, and so was relatively certain of their limitations. These were the areas in which he created his most innovative and unusual spells.

The only group of magical beings that worried Gourenspur were the harpers. Although their magic was not as strong as that of the sorcerers and wizards, it was the only magic that he did not understand. How were they able to travel on the notes of their harps? How had they managed to keep the isle of Spring invisible from even the most powerful magicians? What other powers did they have that might be able to destroy him?

Gourenspur often pondered these questions, and eventually reasoned that perhaps the key to the harpers' magic lay in the isle of Spring. Did they go there to revitalize their powers? That could explain why they often visited the island, and why they kept it cloaked with invisibility. Gourenspur's thoughts became fixed on the idea that if he somehow managed to destroy the island, he would eliminate the harpers' magic, and could once again use his wizardry without fear. He became obsessed with this plan, and thought of nothing else. With the coming of each day, his madness and anger grew. ♪

Chapter 5

It has been said that during this time, Gourenspur often transformed himself into a raven, and flew to the mainland in search of some insight into the harpers' lifestyle that might help him in his evil plot. It was on one of these journeys that he heard a harper talking about his new dagger, which had been forged from the iron ore of the isle of Spring. Gourenspur intuitively perceived that this dagger would be essential to his conquest of the isle. That night, when all was still, his eyes gleamed red and he cast a powerful sleeping spell on the unsuspecting harper, and carried the dagger in his beak back to his island cave.

♪ GOURENSPUR

14

In his secluded shelter, Gourenspur contemplated the importance of his new acquisition. He considered the truth that all man-made objects carry with them aspects of their previous forms and locations. Gourenspur knew how to make these invisible signs apparent through the use of fire and spells of origins. Thus, after many months of experimenting, he was able to cause the dagger blade to hold a mirror-finish that reflected its original home, the isle of Spring. By gazing into the finish of the blade as it glowed red hot in a blazing fire, Gourenspur was able to view one particular clearing on the invisible isle. By casting spells into the vision in the dagger, he was able to transmit his spells to the isle itself.

It was in this manner that Gourenspur had created the mirage of gypsies in the clearing and had trapped Telena. When she first entered the mirage, the power of her harp protected her, its strong magic warding off the evil. However, as soon as she had put down her instrument, his magic had overpowered her, and she was ensnared.

Gourenspur had originally hoped to capture both Brandiswhiere and Telena in the illusion. But the more he thought about it, he found he was glad that Brandiswhiere would be there to oppose him when he attacked the island. Where is the sport in conquest if there is no resistance? He even looked on Brandiswhiere as a bit of a challenge. After all, was he not reputed to be the greatest of the young harpers? He would play with the harper as a cat toys with a mouse before devouring it. He would use one powerful spell, and then sit back and watch Brandiswhiere struggle, and eventually perish.

Gourenspur was confident he could defeat Brandiswhiere, but he did not wish to take the chance of other harpers arriving on the isle to join the battle. To prevent this, he built a powerful wall of magic around the isle of Spring which the harpers would not be able to penetrate. Consequently, Brandiswhiere was isolated from any assistance. He would have to fight alone.

Chapter 6

In the dead of night, Brandiswhiere woke with a start from a fitful sleep filled with turbulent dreams. He felt that someone or something was calling him, yet he heard nothing. He followed the silent, yet etherial voice and was led into a clearing in the forest. All was still, and there, partially hidden beneath the tree where she had left it earlier, was Telena's harp. He disentangled it from the vines that had already entwined themselves in the strings, and set the harp on the grass. A warm breeze blowing through the trees set the strings vibrating, and as the wind and the harp began to play, they formed changing images in Brandiswhiere's mind like a vision.

The harp's notes spoke to him of Telena. He saw her standing like a transparent statue, her hands indicating a warning. A jet-black raven flew by her shoulder, and the vision followed its flight. From the bird's aerial perspective, he saw the forest wither and die; the green lushness turning to brown barrenness, empty of all life. Brandiswhiere's mental images evolved in a kaleidoscopic pattern, and he found himself engaged in battle: sometimes wrestling an unseen force, at other times being attacked by a bearded man with a sword. Yet as the battles faded away, he knew not who had won. The raven returned, bringing billowing black clouds that totally filled Brandiswhiere's mind. ‿♩‿

Gradually, the entire vision grew dim, and he once again saw only the clearing, with Telena's harp glittering in the moonlight. He could not see Telena standing by his side, for she was still invisibly entrapped in Gourenspur's illusion.

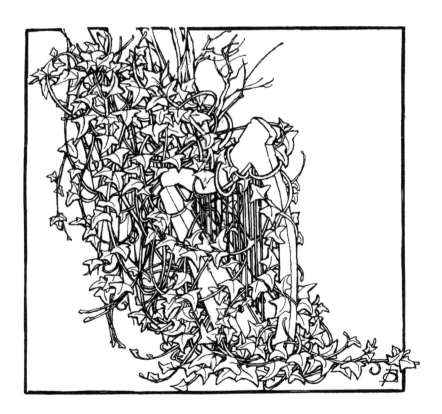

‿♩‿ THE HARPER'S VISION

As the wind waned, the notes of the harp faded away. In the stillness, Brandiswhiere pondered the meaning of the vision. Was it fact? Was it prophecy? Telena was warning him, but of what? He felt certain that the images were somehow symbolic of the evil at work on the island. But what was to come next, and how was he to guard against it?

The first light of day found Brandiswhiere still sitting in the clearing. As the people of the forest arose and started their daily chores, their voices carried over the trees. He could hear them chatting, and calling their cows to come for milking. The morning breeze brought the warm aroma of baking muffins and other delightful smells of breakfast. ♪

Brandiswhiere marveled that this morning appeared to be like all other mornings had been on the isle for generations. Yet this morning was different, for a shadow of evil hung heavily over the forest. He wondered if the calm would soon be shattered by the sharp sounds of battle.

Brandiswhiere heard the men making their way to the fields and orchards to begin their daily work. The forest rang with their songs and their steps as it had every morning for hundreds of years. ♪♪ He wondered how effective they would be if the isle were to be attacked. He knew that they would do all that they could, but most of the responsibility would be on his shoulders. With Telena gone, and no way to summon assistance, he was the only one on the island with magical powers. He felt very isolated and alone.

♪ MORNING CALM
♪♪ FOREST MARCH

Chapter 7

Gourenspur looked into the dagger as it glowed in the flames. He saw Brandiswhiere sitting in the clearing, his harp on his lap, and Telena's harp by his side. It was time to attack. He summoned all his strength and power into one invincible spell, and sent it through the dagger to the isle of perpetual Spring.

The people of the forest felt a sudden disorienting shift in their environment. A windless chill swept across them. All at once it was very cold. Water standing in pans and buckets quickly froze before their startled eyes, and even the waterfall hardened into ice and hung suspended. The thick green grass turned brown, and the brightly colored flowers faded to a pale grey of death.

Next came the wind: a moaning malevolent fury that stripped the trees bare and ripped the petals from the frozen flowers. Gourenspur was turning the lush green life of the isle of Spring into a bleak, barren wasteland.

The sky filled with clouds, and as they darkened the first icy raindrops gave way to snow. Soon a ruthless blizzard howled its rage and filled the air with blinding and biting whiteness. Everything was quickly covered with mounds of snow, and large drifts smothered the leafless trees.

Winter had come to the isle of Spring.

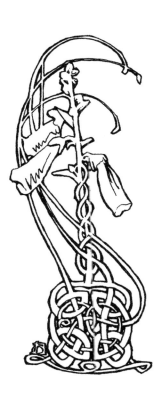

Chapter 8

Brandiswhiere did not move from where he was sitting in the clearing, but knowingly held his position. Remembering the storm clouds of his vision, he realized that this was the danger of which Telena had warned.

The isle was under attack, and its very existence was in jeopardy. What could he do to counteract this destruction? He tried once again to summon help through his harp, but that path was still blocked, and the frigid strings bit into his fingers. The fate of the island and its people rested in his hands and his harp.

As the blizzard raged about him, Brandiswhiere spied one small flower, partially shielded from the demonic wind by his own leg. Although it lay broken and frozen in the snow, it had somehow managed to hold on to its battered and bruised petals. As he gazed at the ravaged flower, he suddenly realized that in Gourenspur's choice of a method of destruction, he had also given the isle its only means of surviving. True enough, the legend said that if Winter ever came, the island would lose its protection of invisibility and be vulnerable to evil. However, it also said that it would then be governed by the same natural laws as the rest of the world. And what is more natural than Winter turning to Spring! If Brandiswhiere could speed up this process, advancing once again to Spring, they would be saved.

Brandiswhiere raised his icy fingers to the brittle strings of his harp, and began to play to this one small, lifeless flower. He played of the Spring sun that shines through the trees on an early morning, melting the snow of a waning Winter. He played of the first blades of grass pushing up through the thinning patches of whiteness, and of ice melting and swelling the cold but running brooks. He played of the warm breezes that blow through the grasses and caress each new petal with gentle embraces. He played of the laughter of children as they run through the meadows. He played of warmth, and Spring, and beauty: he was playing the songs of life!

Gourenspur watched Brandiswhiere in the dagger and wondered what he was trying to accomplish with the music of his harp. It seemed to him that Brandiswhiere had realized it was useless to resist, and was playing to ease his pain of defeat. Perhaps Gourenspur's victory would be easier than he had expected. This was fortunate, for his spell of Winter had drained more of his strength than he had anticipated.

But gradually, Gourenspur perceived that the blizzard's intensity was abating, and he could feel his own power being sucked from him. Was it possible that Brandiswhiere was somehow winning this battle of magic, and sapping his power?

Gourenspur quickly conjured up a lightning bolt with which to strike and kill Brandiswhiere. Obviously, he could take no more chances with this master harper! He raised his arm and hurled the lightning through the dagger. But he did not have enough power to complete the spell at that distance. The lightning bolt turned into a harmless streak of light by the time it reached the clearing.

Gourenspur cried out in rage, and turned away from the vision in the dagger. As he looked out through the entrance of his cave he realized that he could see the isle of Spring clearly through the clouds. The Winter had dissolved its cloak of invisibility, and the island was now fully apparent.

At last Gourenspur could travel to the island. He quickly transformed himself into a raven, and flew toward the isle. But what strange thing was happening? With each flap of his wings, his strength seemed to fade. Could the curse be coming true? Surely Brandiswhiere's magic could not be powerful enough to counter the fury of Winter he had sent upon the island of Spring!

Brandiswhiere played on. Gradually his music turned the blizzard into a gentle rain. The snow began to melt away, and the trees lost their stark frozen appearance. The sun broke through the clouds, and as Brandiswhiere looked up to welcome its warming rays, he saw a large raven flying towards him with menacing cries and extended talons. Brandiswhiere remembered Telena's warning vision, and recognized the bird as the evil that had held the isle in its grip.

Gourenspur landed in the clearing, not far from where Brandiswhiere sat playing, and restored himself to his true human form. Although his powers were greatly depleted, he was able to conjure up a final lightning bolt and hurl it at the harper. This time it hit its mark. With a loud crack, the blue sizzling flame struck Brandiswhiere's harp and shattered it into countless small splinters. Immediately, Winter returned in its vicious intensity, the blizzard raging more desperately than before.

Brandiswhiere felt a sharp pain as his harp was destroyed, as if a part of his being had been vilely torn away and utterly extinguished. He felt much of his power drain from him. But his grief and anger renewed his resolve, and even as Gourenspur screeched a demonic cry of victory, Brandiswhiere reached for Telena's harp which lay amid the strewn rubble of his own. He was far from vanquished, as her gentle instrument became a powerful weapon in his hands. With increasing energy, the music coursed from his determined fingers.

The storm seemed to hesitate, as though assessing Brandiswhiere's strength. For a moment, even the falling snowflakes paused in midair; then a wave of Gourenspur's arm sent the entire focus of the storm crashing directly at Brandiswhiere. He met it headlong, his notes a harmonic onslaught charged with an intensity never heard before. For nowhere in history had anyone played so important a piece. This was to save a land and its people. A song to save himself and to avenge the destruction of a harp which had been so much a part of himself.

With each touch of Telena's harp, he grew stronger and more confident. Suddenly he realized that most of all, he was fighting this battle for her: not the island, not the harp, but Telena. The rage at her loss was the wellspring of his strength in this confrontation. He could feel her in the strings, and in the press of her instrument in the crook of his neck. Oh, if it could be her instead of just her harp. The more he played, the closer she felt. As the magic of Telena's harp surged through him, he once again began to tip the balance in favor of the Spring.

The wind warmed, and its ferocity turned to gentle persistence. Snowdrifts shrank and fed the stream that could once again splash as it ran its course, and lept at last over the waterfall. Buds became apparent on the trees; bulbs sent shoots expectantly skyward. ⌣♩⌣

Brandiswhiere looked down, and there in the shelter of his leg was the flower that had been so badly battered. It now stood straight and tall, bright and colorful as if it were a monument to a great triumph. It was a sign, and Brandiswhiere understood. He played of new life, and it appeared around him, each note bringing a new bud or flower. The dynamic energy from his hands on Telena's harp seemed to compact time, so that the normal cycle of Spring growth took place in a few minutes. He played and created Spring; he played to his lost love.

Gourenspur realized in terror that the curse was coming true. His magic had been countered and the ancient curse was destroying him. He tried to cast a spell to save himself, but all of his power was gone; he was defeated. As he faded into nothingness, Telena began to reappear. She was released from his illusion, and he became engulfed in it. Gourenspur completely vanished, and was consumed by his own magical illusion. Where he had stood, the green grass turned brown, withered, and died. Nothing would ever again grow on that spot where Gourenspur was trapped, invisible, for eternity. The barren spot would be a constant reminder of the evil that Brandiswhiere had vanquished.

⌣♩⌣ METAMORPHOSIS

As the bright sun had begun to warm the island, the people of the forest had come to the edge of the clearing to observe the battle from behind trees. They rejoiced as Telena reappeared, standing directly behind Brandis-whiere. The last glimpse of Gourenspur vanished, and Telena reached out her hand and touched Brandiswhiere on his shoulder. He turned around and beheld his love, restored again by his music and the magic of her own harp.

Spring had truly returned to the island. ◡♩◡

◡♩◡ BRANDISWHIERE'S TRIUMPHANT RETURN

THE LEGEND

music by SYLVIA WOODS

MODERATELY

26

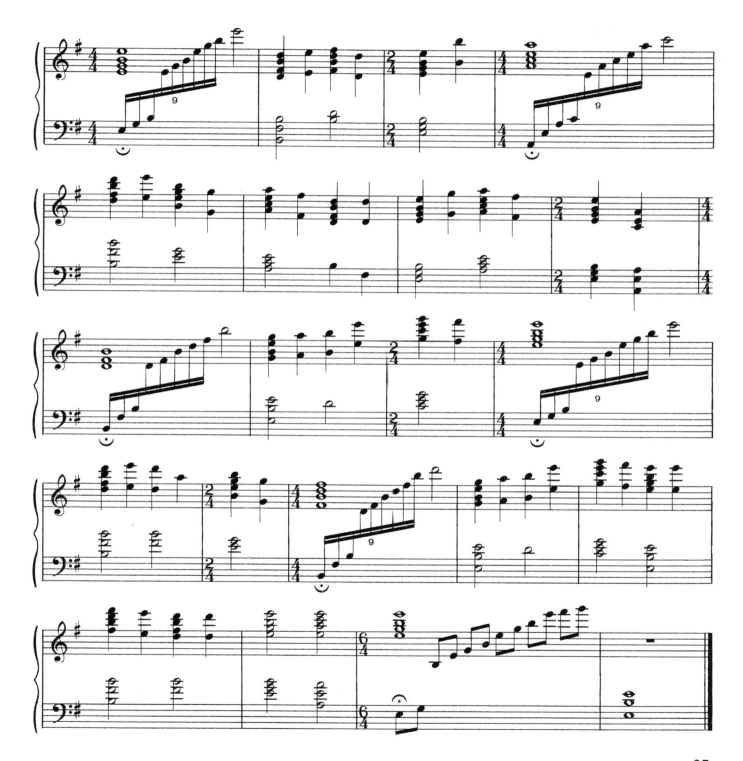

27

IN THE FOREST

music by SYLVIA WOODS

FLOWINGLY, WALTZ-LIKE

30

DIALOGUE WITH A BROOK

music by SYLVIA WOODS

Fine

Slow and rubato

a tempo

D .S al Fine

33

LAMENT

music by SYLVIA WOODS

MOURNFULLY

35

GYPSY MIRAGE

music by SYLVIA WOODS

37

GOURENSPUR

SLOWLY

(All A's are sharp)

music by SYLVIA WOODS

Harshly

41

THE HARPER'S VISION

music by SYLVIA WOODS

PEACEFULLY

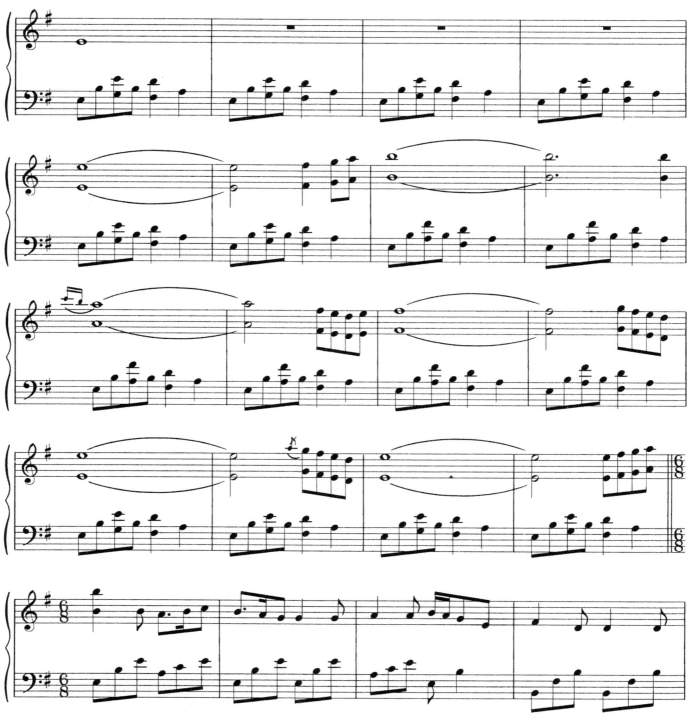

44

45

46

47

48

MORNING CALM

music by SYLVIA WOODS

SMOOTHLY, EXTREMELY RUBATO

49

accel.

FOREST MARCH

music by SYLVIA WOODS

MARCH-LIKE

53

METAMORPHOSIS

music by SYLVIA WOODS

LEISURELY

55

BRANDISWHIERE'S
TRIUMPHANT RETURN

HAPPILY, IN A MARCH TEMPO
(All F's are sharp)

music by SYLVIA WOODS

59

Additional Harp Music by Sylvia Woods

BOOKS

Beauty and the Beast
Chanukah Music
50 Christmas Carols
John Denver Love Songs
76 Disney Songs
Favorites from the 50s
Gecko Tails
Groovy Songs of the 60s
Harp Fingering Fundamentals
Four Holiday Favorites
Hymns and Wedding Music
Irish Dance Tunes
50 Irish Melodies
Jesu, Joy of Man's Desiring
Lennon and McCartney
Music Theory & Arranging Techniques
40 O'Carolan Tunes
Pachelbel's Canon
22 Romantic Songs
52 Scottish Songs
Teach Yourself to Play the Folk Harp
Andrew Lloyd Webber
The Wizard of Oz

SHEET MUSIC

A Charlie Brown Christmas
A Thousand Years
All of Me
All the Pretty Little Horses
America Medley
Music from Disney-Pixar's Brave
Bring Him Home and Castle on a Cloud
from Les Miserables
Two Christmas Medleys
Dead Poets Society
Everything
Fields of Gold
Fireflies

Flower Duet
Music from Disney's Frozen
Game of Thrones
Hallelujah
Happy
Happy Birthday to You
Harpers are Not Bizarre
Here Comes the Sun
House at Pooh Corner
How Does a Moment Last Forever
In the Bleak Midwinter
Into the West from Lord of the Rings
It's a Beautiful Day
La La Land
Lava
Marry Me
Mary Did You Know?
My Heart Will Go On from Titanic
Over the Rainbow from Wizard of Oz
Perfect
Photograph
Safe & Sound
Say Something
Simple Gifts
Spiritual Medley
Stairway to Heaven
Star-Spangled Banner
Stay with Me
Music from Disney's Tangled
That Night in Bethlehem
Unchained Melody
Unforgettable
Theme from Disney-Pixar's Up
The Water is Wide
Wedding March by Mendelssohn
When You Say You Love Me
While My Guitar Gently Weeps
Winter Bells
Wondrous Love

Available from your local harp store or from
Sylvia Woods Harp Center at www.harpcenter.com/sylviamusic